HOW TO MASTER WORK LIFE BALANCE

Boost Productivity, Develop Healthy Relationships, Manage Stress and Burnout, and Maintain Lifelong Happiness.

PRADIP DAS

© Copyright 2024 - All rights reserved.

The content contained within this book may not be reproduced, duplicated, or transmitted without direct written permission from the author or the publisher. Under no circumstances will any blame or legal responsibility be held against the publisher, or author, for any damages, reparation, or monetary loss due to the information contained within this book. Either directly or indirectly.

Legal Notice:

This book is copyright protected. This book is only for personal use. You cannot amend, distribute, sell, use, quote or paraphrase any part, or the content within this book, without the consent of the author or publisher.

Disclaimer Notice:

Please note the information contained within this document is for educational and entertainment purposes only. All effort has been executed to present accurate, up to date, and reliable, complete information. No warranties of any kind are declared or implied. Readers acknowledge that the author is not engaging in the rendering of legal, financial, medical or professional advice. The content within this book has been derived from various sources. Please consult a licensed professional before attempting any techniques outlined in this book.

By reading this document, the reader agrees that under no circumstances is the author responsible for any losses, direct or indirect, which are incurred as a result of the use of information contained within this document, including, but not limited to, — errors, omissions, or inaccuracies.

*Please scan for the other books of the **"Life Mastery"** Series.*

Table of Contents

Table of Contents 4
Introduction 5
Understanding Work-Life Balance 10
Strategies for Achieving Work-Life Balance
.... 17
Managing Stress and Burnout 28
Creating Boundaries 38
Nurturing Relationships 45
Maximizing Productivity 56
Flexibility and Adaptability 68
Self-Reflection and Growth 78
Implementing Work-Life Balance 87
Final Thoughts 94

Introduction

Finding a harmonious balance between work and personal life has become increasingly challenging. As demands on our time and attention continue to grow, many of us find ourselves struggling to juggle the responsibilities of our careers with the desire to nurture our personal relationships, pursue hobbies, and take care of our own well-being. The quest for work-life balance can often feel like an uphill battle, leaving us feeling overwhelmed, stressed, and disconnected from the things that truly matter.

But what if achieving work-life balance wasn't just a distant dream, but a tangible reality within our reach? What if we could learn to navigate the complexities of modern life with grace and ease, finding fulfillment and joy in both our professional and personal endeavors? This book, "How to Master Work-Life Balance," is designed to help you do just that.

What is Work-Life Balance?

Work-life balance means having enough time for work and personal life without feeling overwhelmed or stressed. It's about finding harmony between your job and everything else you want to do, like spending time with family, pursuing hobbies, or just relaxing.

Anupama, a hardworking mom who loves her job as a nurse. She spends long hours at the hospital, caring for patients and making sure everything runs smoothly. But as much as she loves her job, Sarah also wants to be there for her family. She wants to attend her daughter's school events, have dinner with her husband, and just unwind at home. However, because of her demanding work schedule, Anupama often finds herself rushing from one thing to the next, feeling exhausted and guilty for not spending enough time with her loved ones. This lack of balance takes a toll on her well-being and leaves her feeling stressed and overwhelmed.

Anupama's story illustrates the importance of work-life balance. Without it, we risk burning out and missing out on the things that truly matter in life. Achieving balance means finding ways to manage our time effectively, prioritize what's important, and create boundaries between work and personal life. It's about making choices that allow us to thrive both professionally and personally, leading happier, healthier, and more fulfilling lives.

Importance of Achieving Work-Life Balance:

Achieving work-life balance isn't just about finding more time for leisure and relaxation; it's about creating a sustainable lifestyle that supports our overall well-being and happiness. When we neglect to prioritize balance in our lives, we risk falling victim to burnout, stress, and even tragedy.

Hardik, a dedicated professional who poured all his time and energy into his career, neglecting his relationships and personal interests in the process. Despite his success in the corporate world, Hardik's relentless pursuit of professional excellence came at a steep cost. He spent long hours at the office, sacrificing quality time with his family and friends. Eventually, the stress and strain of his demanding job took a toll on his health, leading to chronic fatigue, anxiety, and depression.

Tragically, Hardik's obsession with work ultimately led to the breakdown of his marriage, estrangement from his children, and a profound sense of loneliness and emptiness. Despite his achievements in his career, John realized too late that true fulfillment and happiness cannot be found solely in professional success. His story serves as a poignant reminder of the importance of achieving a healthy balance between work and personal life.

By prioritizing work-life balance, we can avoid the pitfalls that befell John and countless others like him. When we make time for the people and activities that bring us joy and fulfillment outside of work, we cultivate stronger relationships, improve our mental and physical health, and enhance our overall quality of life. Achieving work-life balance isn't just a luxury; it's a necessity for our well-being and happiness.

About The Book

In this book, you will find a holistic approach to achieving work-life balance that goes beyond simple time management techniques.

Imagine a tightrope walker performing high above the ground. Each step requires precision, focus, and balance. In the same way, balancing work and life is like walking a tightrope. If you lean too far in one direction, you risk losing your footing and falling.

You will come to know how to find that delicate equilibrium, allowing you to navigate the challenges of both work and personal life with confidence and grace.

You will gain insights into how to identify your priorities, set boundaries, and create habits that support a balanced lifestyle. Whether you're a busy professional, a dedicated parent, or someone simply seeking a more fulfilling and balanced existence, the insights and wisdom contained within these pages will empower you to take control of your time, your priorities, and ultimately, your life.

So, whether you are struggling to juggle the demands of work and family, feeling like you're constantly running on empty, or simply seeking a more fulfilling and balanced existence, this book will provide you with the tools and guidance you need to thrive in all areas of your life.

Understanding Work-Life Balance

Work-life balance is a term that's often thrown around, but what does it really mean? At its core, work-life balance refers to the equilibrium between the time and energy we devote to our work and the time we dedicate to our personal lives. It's about finding a healthy blend between our professional responsibilities and our personal pursuits, allowing us to thrive both in our careers and in our relationships outside of work.

To understand the importance of work-life balance, let's consider a hypothetical example: the Smith family. Mr. Smith is a dedicated employee who works long hours at his demanding job, often sacrificing time with his family to meet work deadlines and attend meetings. Mrs. Smith, on the other hand, is a stay-at-home parent who shoulders the bulk of the household responsibilities, from managing the household finances to caring for their children.

Despite their best intentions, the Smiths find themselves caught in a vicious cycle of work and domestic duties, leaving little time for meaningful connection as a family. As weeks turn into months and months into years, the strain of their hectic schedules begins to take its toll. Mr. Smith experiences burnout from the relentless demands of his job, while Mrs. Smith feels isolated and overwhelmed by the responsibilities of managing the household single-handedly.

Unfortunately, their family's struggle with work-life balance comes to a head when they receive news of a family emergency. Mr. Smith's elderly parents, who live in another city, fall ill, requiring immediate care and attention. However, Mr. Smith's demanding job leaves him unable to take time off to be with his parents, while Mrs. Smith is left to manage the household and care for their children alone. In the midst of this crisis, the Smiths realize that their relentless pursuit of career success has come at the expense of their family's well-being and happiness.

This scenario of work-life balance is very much prevent in the families. When we prioritize our careers at the expense of our personal lives, we risk damaging our relationships, our health, and our overall sense of fulfillment. Achieving work-life balance isn't just about clocking in and out of work—it's about creating space for the things that truly matter, whether it's spending quality time with loved ones, pursuing hobbies and interests, or simply taking time to recharge and rejuvenate.

Common Misconceptions and Challenges

Achieving a healthy work-life balance is often seen as an elusive goal, with many misconceptions and challenges along the way. Let's explore some of the most common misconceptions and challenges people face when striving to balance their professional and personal lives.

Misconception: Work-Life Balance Means Equal Time for Work and Personal Life.

Many people mistakenly believe that achieving work-life balance means spending an equal amount of time on work and personal life activities. However, true balance is about prioritizing and allocating time based on individual needs and priorities.

Challenge: Difficulty Setting Boundaries Between Work and Personal Life.

With the rise of remote work and digital connectivity, many people struggle to establish clear boundaries between their professional and personal lives. This can lead to work encroaching on personal time, resulting in increased stress and decreased satisfaction.

Misconception: Work-Life Balance is a One-Time Achievement.

Some people mistakenly view work-life balance as a destination to be reached rather than an ongoing journey. They believe that once they achieve balance, they can maintain it indefinitely without effort.

Challenge: Guilt Associated with Prioritizing Personal Time Over Work.

Many individuals feel guilty when prioritizing personal time over work responsibilities, fearing it will negatively impact their career prospects or productivity.

Navigating these misconceptions and challenges requires self-awareness, intentionality, and a willingness to prioritize what truly matters. By setting realistic expectations, establishing clear boundaries, and regularly reassessing priorities, individuals can strive to achieve a more balanced and fulfilling life.

Work-life balance is not a destination to be reached, but a journey to be embraced—one that requires constant effort, adaptation, and self-care.

Identifying Personal Priorities and Values

Understanding work-life balance starts with a deep exploration of our personal priorities and values. These are the guiding principles that shape our decisions, actions, and ultimately, our sense of fulfillment in life. By taking the time to identify what truly matters to us, we can align our choices with our core values and create a more harmonious and satisfying balance between our work and personal lives.

Consider the story of Sunita, a dedicated professional who worked long hours to climb the corporate ladder. While she excelled in her career, her relentless pursuit of success came at a cost. She often missed important family events, neglected her health, and sacrificed quality time with her loved ones. Despite her achievements at work, Sunita's personal life suffered, leading to strained relationships and feelings of emptiness and regret.

To avoid the pitfalls of neglecting personal priorities, it's essential to take stock of what truly matters most to us. This involves reflecting on our values, aspirations, and the kind of life we envision for ourselves. For some, family may be the top priority, while others may place greater emphasis on career advancement, health, or personal growth.

One way to identify personal priorities is by creating a values inventory. Start by listing down the things that bring you joy, fulfillment, and a sense of purpose. This could include spending quality time with family, pursuing hobbies and passions, contributing to your community, or maintaining good health. Reflect on each item and consider how it aligns with your overall values and long-term goals.

Once you've identified your personal priorities, the next step is to align your choices and actions with these values. This may involve setting boundaries at work, prioritizing time for self-care and family, and saying no to activities or commitments that don't align with your core values.

Identifying personal priorities and values is a crucial first step towards achieving work-life balance. By understanding what truly matters to us, we can make intentional choices that align with our core values and lead to greater fulfillment and happiness in both our professional and personal lives.

Strategies for Achieving Work-Life Balance

Setting Realistic Goals and Expectations

In our quest for work-life balance, one of the most crucial strategies we can employ is setting realistic goals and expectations. While it's important to dream big and aim high, it's equally important to ground our aspirations in reality and set achievable objectives that align with our values, priorities, and resources.

Assess Your Current Situation: Before diving into setting goals, take some time to assess your current situation. Reflect on your work commitments, personal responsibilities, and lifestyle preferences. Consider what's working well and what areas could use improvement. By understanding where you stand, you'll be better equipped to set goals that address your specific needs and circumstances.

Define Your Priorities: Identify the key areas of your life that are most important to you. This could include your career, relationships, health, hobbies, or personal growth. Clarify your values and determine what matters most in each of these areas. By defining your priorities, you can focus your time and energy on the things that truly matter to you, rather than spreading yourself too thin trying to do it all.

Set Goals: When setting goals, follow the SMART criteria: Specific, Measurable, Achievable, Relevant, and Time-bound. Be clear and specific about what you want to achieve, and establish measurable metrics to track your progress. Ensure that your goals are realistic and attainable given your current circumstances. Make sure they align with your priorities and are relevant to your overall vision for work-life balance. Finally, set deadlines or milestones to keep yourself accountable and motivated.

Break It Down: Large goals can feel overwhelming, so break them down into smaller, more manageable tasks or sub-goals. This will make them less daunting and easier to tackle. Create a step-by-step plan outlining the actions you need to take to achieve each goal. Celebrate your progress along the way, and adjust your plan as needed based on feedback and changing circumstances.

Be Flexible and Adaptive: While it's important to set goals and work towards them, it's equally important to remain flexible and adaptive in the face of unexpected challenges or setbacks. Life is unpredictable, and things don't always go according to plan. Instead of becoming discouraged, view setbacks as learning opportunities and opportunities to adjust your approach. Be willing to reassess your goals and expectations as needed to stay on track and maintain balance in your life.

Practice Self-Compassion: Finally, be kind to yourself throughout the goal-setting process. It's okay to not have everything figured out, and it's normal to experience setbacks along the way. Practice self-compassion and acknowledge your efforts and progress, no matter how small. Remember that work-life balance is a journey, not a destination, and that it's okay to recalibrate your goals and expectations as you go.

Prioritizing Tasks and Activities:

It is easy to feel overwhelmed by the sheer number of tasks and activities vying for our attention. From work deadlines to household chores to social commitments, the list of things to do can seem never-ending. However, learning to prioritize tasks and activities is key to achieving work-life balance and managing our time effectively.

Identify Your Priorities: The first step in prioritizing tasks is to identify what truly matters to you. Take some time to reflect on your values, goals, and responsibilities, both at work and in your personal life. What are the most important tasks that will help you move closer to your objectives? By clarifying your priorities, you can focus your time and energy on the things that matter most.

Use the Eisenhower Matrix: The Eisenhower Matrix is a simple yet powerful tool for prioritizing tasks based on their urgency and importance. Divide your tasks into four categories: urgent and important, important but not urgent, urgent but not important, and neither urgent nor important. Focus on tackling tasks in the urgent and important quadrant first, followed by those in the important but not urgent quadrant.

Set Goals: When setting goals, make sure they align with your priorities and are realistic given your time and resources. Break down larger goals into smaller, actionable steps, and assign deadlines to keep yourself accountable. This will help you stay focused and make progress towards your objectives.

Learn to Say No: One of the biggest challenges in prioritizing tasks is learning to say no to things that don't align with your priorities or goals. While it can be tempting to say yes to every request that comes your way, overcommitting yourself can lead to burnout and overwhelm. Practice setting boundaries and politely declining requests that don't serve your best interests.

Delegate and Outsource: You don't have to do everything yourself. Learn to delegate tasks to others who are better suited to handle them or outsource tasks that can be done more efficiently by someone else. Delegating not only frees up your time for more important activities but also empowers others to contribute their skills and expertise.

Use Time Blocking: Time blocking involves scheduling specific blocks of time for different tasks and activities throughout your day. Allocate dedicated time slots for work, personal errands, exercise, relaxation, and family time. By sticking to a structured schedule, you can ensure that all your priorities are given the attention they deserve.

Practice the Two-Minute Rule: The Two-Minute Rule states that if a task can be completed in two minutes or less, you should do it immediately. Instead of putting off small tasks that can be done quickly, tackle them right away to prevent them from piling up and causing unnecessary stress.

Review and Adjust Regularly: Priorities can change over time, so it's important to regularly review and adjust your task list accordingly. Take time at the end of each day or week to reflect on your progress, evaluate what's working well, and make any necessary adjustments to your priorities and goals.

By prioritizing tasks and activities effectively, you can create more time and space for the things that truly matter in your life. With practice and consistency, you can achieve greater balance, productivity, and fulfillment in both your work and personal endeavors.

Time Management Techniques for Achieving Work-Life Balance:

In the pursuit of work-life balance, effective time management is essential. By learning to manage your time wisely, you can create space for both your professional responsibilities and personal pursuits. Here are some simple yet powerful time management techniques to help you achieve greater balance in your life:

Practice Time Management Techniques:

Time management techniques such as the Pomodoro Technique, the Eisenhower Matrix, and the 80/20 Rule can help you maximize your productivity and efficiency.

Experiment with different techniques to find what works best for you, and incorporate them into your daily routine.

Limit Distractions:

Identify common distractions that hinder your productivity, such as social media, email, or unnecessary meetings. Take proactive steps to minimize or eliminate these distractions.

Consider using productivity tools and apps that help you stay focused and block out distractions during designated work periods.

Practice Mindfulness:

Mindfulness techniques, such as meditation and deep breathing exercises, can help you stay present and focused in the moment. Incorporate mindfulness practices into your daily routine to reduce stress and increase mental clarity.

Take short mindfulness breaks throughout your day to reset and recharge, allowing you to approach tasks with renewed energy and focus.

By implementing these time management techniques into your daily life, you can create a more balanced and fulfilling existence, where work and personal life coexist harmoniously. Remember that achieving work-life balance is an ongoing process, and it requires dedication, intentionality, and a willingness to adapt as needed. With time management as your ally, you can take control of your schedule, reduce stress, and live a life filled with purpose and joy.

Delegation and outsourcing

Delegation and outsourcing are two powerful strategies that can help you achieve better work-life balance by lightening your workload and freeing up time for the things that matter most.

Delegation involves assigning tasks or responsibilities to others who have the skills and capability to handle them. By delegating tasks that are time-consuming or outside your area of expertise, you can focus your energy on more important priorities. For example, if you're a manager, you could delegate administrative tasks to an assistant, allowing you to spend more time on strategic planning and decision-making.

Outsourcing, on the other hand, involves hiring external professionals or services to handle certain aspects of your work or personal life. This could include outsourcing tasks like accounting, IT support, or house cleaning. By outsourcing tasks that are repetitive or specialized, you can save time and energy that can be invested in activities that bring you joy and fulfillment.

When delegating or outsourcing tasks, it's important to consider the following factors:

Identify your priorities: Determine which tasks are essential for you to handle personally and which can be delegated or outsourced. Focus your time and energy on tasks that align with your goals and values.

Assess skills and capabilities: Delegate tasks to individuals who have the skills and knowledge to complete them effectively. When outsourcing, choose reputable professionals or service providers who specialize in the task at hand.

Communicate clearly: Clearly communicate your expectations, deadlines, and any relevant information to the person or team you're delegating to. Provide necessary training or guidance to ensure they understand the task and can complete it successfully.

Set boundaries: Establish boundaries and limits on what tasks you're willing to delegate or outsource. Be realistic about what you can reasonably handle on your own and don't overextend yourself.

Monitor progress: Stay informed about the progress of delegated tasks and provide feedback or guidance as needed. Regular check-ins can help ensure tasks are completed on time and to your satisfaction.

Be open to feedback: Encourage open communication and feedback from those you delegate to or outsource tasks to. Be willing to listen to their suggestions and make adjustments as needed to improve processes and outcomes.

By effectively delegating and outsourcing tasks, you can create more time and space in your life for the things that bring you joy and fulfillment. Whether it's spending quality time with loved ones, pursuing hobbies and interests, or simply taking time to relax and recharge, these strategies can help you achieve better work-life balance and live a more fulfilling life.

Managing Stress and Burnout

Stress and burnout have become all too common nowadays. From the pressures of work to the demands of daily life, it's easy to feel overwhelmed and stretched thin. But how do you know when stress is becoming too much to handle, and when it's turning into burnout? Understanding the signs and symptoms is the first step towards managing stress and preventing burnout.

Physical Symptoms:

Pay attention to your body. Are you experiencing headaches, muscle tension, or stomach problems? These can be signs that stress is taking a toll on your physical health.

Notice any changes in your sleep patterns. Are you having trouble falling asleep or staying asleep? Or maybe you're sleeping too much? Disrupted sleep can be a sign of stress and burnout.

Keep an eye on your appetite. Are you eating more than usual, or have you lost your appetite altogether? Changes in eating habits can be a red flag for stress-related issues.

Emotional Symptoms:

Monitor your mood. Are you feeling irritable, anxious, or overwhelmed? Do you find yourself crying more often or feeling emotionally numb? These are all signs that stress is affecting your emotional well-being.

Pay attention to changes in your behavior. Are you withdrawing from social activities or snapping at loved ones? These behaviors can indicate that stress is impacting your relationships and overall happiness.

Notice any feelings of hopelessness or despair. If you're experiencing a sense of dread or feeling like you can't cope with life's challenges, it may be a sign that burnout is looming.

Cognitive Symptoms:

Watch for difficulty concentrating or making decisions. Are you finding it hard to focus on tasks or remember things? This could be a sign that stress is impairing your cognitive function.

Notice any negative thoughts or self-talk. Are you constantly criticizing yourself or dwelling on mistakes? These thought patterns can contribute to stress and make it harder to cope with challenges.

Pay attention to any feelings of detachment or disengagement. If you're feeling disconnected from your work or your relationships, it may be a sign that burnout is setting in.

Behavioral Symptoms:

Keep track of changes in your work habits. Are you procrastinating more than usual or struggling to meet deadlines? Are you taking on too much or neglecting important tasks? These behaviors can indicate that stress is impacting your work performance.

Notice any changes in your coping mechanisms. Are you turning to unhealthy habits like smoking, drinking, or overeating to cope with stress? These behaviors may provide temporary relief but can ultimately make stress worse in the long run.

Pay attention to any changes in your leisure activities. Are you no longer enjoying the things you used to love? Are you neglecting hobbies or activities that bring you joy? This can be a sign that stress is draining your energy and enthusiasm.

By recognizing these signs and symptoms of stress and burnout, you can take proactive steps to manage your stress levels and prevent burnout before it takes a toll on your health and well-being. From practicing self-care and setting boundaries to seeking support from friends, family, or a professional, there are many strategies you can use to cope with stress and build resilience in the face of life's challenges. Remember, you don't have to face stress and burnout alone. With the right tools and support, you can reclaim control of your life and find greater balance and fulfillment.

Coping Mechanisms and Stress Management

In today's world, it's common to feel overwhelmed by the pressures of work, relationships, and other responsibilities. When stress becomes too much to handle, it can lead to burnout – a state of physical, emotional, and mental exhaustion. However, there are strategies and coping mechanisms that can help us manage stress effectively and prevent burnout from taking over our lives.

Recognizing Stress: The first step in managing stress is to recognize when we're feeling overwhelmed. This could manifest as feelings of irritability, anxiety, or physical symptoms like headaches or fatigue. By acknowledging our stressors, we can begin to take steps to address them.

Deep Breathing and Relaxation Techniques: Deep breathing exercises and relaxation techniques can help calm the mind and body, reducing feelings of stress and anxiety. Techniques like deep breathing, progressive muscle relaxation, and guided imagery can be practiced anywhere and anytime to promote relaxation.

Setting Boundaries: Setting boundaries is essential for managing stress and preventing burnout. This may involve saying no to additional responsibilities, delegating tasks when possible, and prioritizing self-care activities. By setting boundaries, we can protect our time and energy and prevent ourselves from becoming overwhelmed.

Time Management: Effective time management is crucial for reducing stress and increasing productivity. This may involve creating to-do lists, prioritizing tasks, and breaking large projects into smaller, manageable steps. By managing our time effectively, we can reduce feelings of overwhelm and accomplish more in less time.

Seeking Support: It's important to remember that we don't have to navigate stress alone. Seeking support from friends, family, or a professional therapist can provide valuable perspective and help us cope with difficult emotions. Talking to someone we trust can offer comfort and validation during challenging times.

Practicing Self-Care: Self-care activities are essential for maintaining mental and emotional well-being. This may include activities like exercise, meditation, spending time in nature, or engaging in hobbies and interests. Taking time for ourselves allows us to recharge and replenish our energy reserves, making us better equipped to handle stress.

Adopting a Positive Mindset: Cultivating a positive mindset can help us cope with stress and adversity more effectively. This may involve practicing gratitude, focusing on the present moment, and reframing negative thoughts into more positive ones. By adopting a positive outlook, we can build resilience and bounce back from setbacks more easily.

Avoiding Unhealthy Coping Mechanisms: While it may be tempting to turn to unhealthy coping mechanisms like substance abuse or excessive screen time, these behaviors can ultimately aggravate stress and lead to burnout. Instead, focus on adopting healthy coping mechanisms that promote relaxation and well-being.

Taking Breaks: Taking regular breaks throughout the day is essential for managing stress and preventing burnout. Whether it's a short walk outside, a brief meditation session, or a quick chat with a colleague, taking breaks allows us to recharge and return to our tasks feeling refreshed and focused.

Knowing When to Seek Help: If stress becomes overwhelming and begins to interfere with daily life, it's important to seek help from a qualified mental health professional. They can provide support, guidance, and resources to help manage stress and prevent burnout.

By incorporating these coping mechanisms and stress management techniques into our daily lives, we can reduce feelings of overwhelm, increase resilience, and cultivate a greater sense of well-being. Managing stress is an ongoing process, and it's okay to ask for help when we need it.

Importance of self-care and relaxation

Stress and burnout have become all too common. Whether it's the demands of work, family responsibilities, or personal challenges, we often find ourselves feeling overwhelmed and exhausted. That's where self-care and relaxation come in. These practices are not just luxuries; they are essential tools for managing stress and preventing burnout.

Self-care is all about taking care of yourself, both mentally and physically. It means making time for activities that nourish your body, mind, and soul. This could be as simple as taking a walk in nature, practicing meditation or mindfulness, or enjoying a hobby you love. The key is to prioritize yourself and your well-being, even when life gets busy.

Relaxation is another crucial aspect of managing stress. When we're stressed, our bodies go into "fight or flight" mode, releasing hormones like cortisol and adrenaline that can wreak havoc on our health. Relaxation techniques help counteract this response, activating the body's relaxation response and promoting feelings of calm and tranquility. This can include deep breathing exercises, progressive muscle relaxation, or simply taking time to unwind and do something you enjoy.

The importance of self-care and relaxation cannot be overstated. Not only do these practices help reduce stress in the moment, but they also have long-term benefits for our physical and mental health. Research has shown that regular self-care can improve mood, boost immune function, and even lower the risk of chronic diseases like heart disease and diabetes. Similarly, relaxation techniques have been linked to lower blood pressure, improved sleep, and reduced symptoms of anxiety and depression.

Incorporating self-care and relaxation into your daily routine doesn't have to be complicated or time-consuming. Even small acts of self-care, like taking a few moments to breathe deeply or enjoying a cup of tea, can make a big difference in how you feel. The key is to make self-care a priority and to find activities that resonate with you personally. Whether it's spending time in nature, practicing yoga, or indulging in a favorite hobby, the important thing is to find what works for you and to make time for it regularly.

By prioritizing self-care and relaxation, you're not only taking care of yourself, but you're also better equipping yourself to handle the challenges and stresses of life. So take a moment to pause, breathe, and give yourself the care and attention you deserve. Your mind, body, and spirit will thank you for it.

Creating Boundaries

It is easy for the lines between work and personal life to become blurred. With the constant connectivity of smartphones and the pressure to always be "on," many of us find ourselves struggling to find a balance between our professional responsibilities and our personal well-being. However, establishing clear boundaries between work and personal life is essential for maintaining our mental, emotional, and physical health.

Understanding the Importance of Boundaries: Before we go into how to establish boundaries, let's first understand why they're important. Boundaries serve as a protective barrier between our work and personal lives, allowing us to maintain a sense of autonomy, control, and balance. Without boundaries, we risk becoming overwhelmed, burnt out, and disconnected from the things that truly matter to us.

Identifying Your Priorities: The first step in establishing boundaries is to identify your priorities. What matters most to you in your personal life? What are your career goals and aspirations? By clarifying your priorities, you can determine where to allocate your time, energy, and attention, and set boundaries accordingly.

Setting Clear Work Hours: One effective way to establish boundaries is to set clear work hours. Determine when you will start and end your workday, and stick to those hours as much as possible. Communicate your work schedule to your colleagues, supervisors, and clients, so they know when you are available and when you are not.

Creating Physical and Emotional Separation: Create physical and emotional separation between your work and personal spaces. Designate a specific area in your home for work, such as a home office or a designated workspace. When you're in this space, focus solely on work-related tasks, and when you're outside of it, allow yourself to disconnect and unwind.

Establishing Technology Boundaries: Technology can be a double-edged sword when it comes to work-life balance. While it offers flexibility and convenience, it can also lead to constant connectivity and intrusion into our personal lives. Set boundaries around technology use by turning off work-related notifications outside of work hours, designating specific times for checking email and messages, and unplugging from screens during designated personal time.

Communicating Your Boundaries: Effective communication is key to establishing and maintaining boundaries. Clearly communicate your boundaries to your colleagues, supervisors, and clients, and don't be afraid to assertively enforce them when necessary. Remember, your boundaries are there to protect your well-being, and it's okay to advocate for yourself.

Prioritizing Self-Care: Finally, prioritize self-care as an essential component of maintaining healthy boundaries. Make time for activities that nourish your mind, body, and soul, whether it's exercising, spending time with loved ones, pursuing hobbies, or simply relaxing and unwinding. When you take care of yourself, you're better equipped to show up as your best self in both your work and personal life.

By implementing these strategies and techniques, you can create a healthier, more balanced relationship between your work and personal life, allowing you to thrive in both areas. Establishing boundaries is not selfish – it's an act of self-preservation and self-respect. So, take ownership of your time, honor your priorities, and create a life that aligns with your values and aspirations.

Setting limits on work hours and availability

Setting limits on work hours and availability is essential for maintaining a healthy balance between our professional and personal lives. In today's digital age, where technology allows us to be constantly connected, it can be challenging to establish clear boundaries between work and personal time. However, by setting specific limits on when we work and when we are available, we can prevent burnout, reduce stress, and create more time for the things that matter most to us.

One effective way to set limits on work hours is by establishing a fixed schedule. This means defining set start and end times for your workday and sticking to them as much as possible. By having a predetermined schedule, you can ensure that you allocate sufficient time for work tasks while also allowing for dedicated periods of rest and relaxation. Additionally, having a set schedule can help you manage expectations with colleagues and clients, making it clear when you are available for meetings, calls, and other work-related activities.

Another important aspect of setting limits on work hours is learning to prioritize tasks effectively. Rather than trying to do everything at once, it's essential to identify the most critical tasks and focus on completing them first. This may require delegating less important tasks to others or saying no to additional commitments that could overwhelm your schedule. By prioritizing tasks and managing your workload effectively, you can avoid overextending yourself and ensure that you have enough time for both work and personal activities.

In addition to setting limits on work hours, it's also crucial to establish boundaries around your availability outside of work. This means being clear about when you are accessible to colleagues and clients and when you need time for yourself and your loved ones. One way to do this is by setting specific "off" hours during which you do not respond to work-related emails, calls, or messages. By communicating these boundaries to others, you can avoid the expectation of constant availability and create space for relaxation and rejuvenation.

Furthermore, setting limits on work hours and availability requires effective communication with colleagues, supervisors, and clients. It's essential to be assertive in expressing your needs and boundaries while also being respectful of others' time and priorities. By having open and honest conversations about your availability and work expectations, you can establish mutual understanding and cooperation, leading to better work-life balance for everyone involved.

Setting limits on work hours and availability is crucial for maintaining a healthy balance between work and personal life. By establishing a fixed schedule, prioritizing tasks effectively, and communicating boundaries with others, we can prevent burnout, reduce stress, and create more time for the things that bring us joy and fulfillment. So, take control of your schedule, set clear boundaries, and prioritize your well-being. Your work-life balance depends on it.

Please check the Book Series of
"The Art of Living"

Nurturing Relationships

In our busy schedule, it can be tough to find the right balance between spending time with our family, friends, and colleagues. Each of these relationships is important, but finding the time to nurture them all can feel like a challenge. Here are some simple tips to help you strike a healthy balance:

Prioritize Your Relationships: Start by identifying which relationships are most important to you. Your family, close friends, and trusted colleagues are likely at the top of your list. Once you know who matters most, you can prioritize your time accordingly.

Schedule Quality Time: Just like you schedule important work meetings or appointments, make time in your calendar for quality time with your loved ones. Whether it's a weekly dinner with family, a coffee date with a friend, or a team-building activity with colleagues, setting aside dedicated time ensures that you prioritize these relationships.

Be Present: When you're spending time with your family, friends, or colleagues, be fully present in the moment. Put away your phone, resist the urge to check emails, and focus on engaging with the people around you. Active listening and genuine conversations can strengthen your connections and make the time spent together more meaningful.

Set Boundaries: While it's important to nurture your relationships, it's also essential to set boundaries to protect your time and energy. Learn to say no to commitments that don't align with your priorities, and don't feel guilty about prioritizing self-care when needed.

Find Balance in Flexibility: Flexibility is key when it comes to balancing your time between family, friends, and colleagues. Some days, work commitments may take precedence, while other days, you may need to prioritize family or personal time. Embrace the ebb and flow of life, and be willing to adjust your schedule as needed.

Incorporate Social Activities: Look for opportunities to combine socializing with other activities you enjoy. For example, you could invite friends to join you for a workout or a hobby you're passionate about. This allows you to nurture your relationships while also pursuing your interests.

Communicate Openly: Effective communication is essential for maintaining healthy relationships. Be open and honest with your family, friends, and colleagues about your priorities and commitments. If you're feeling overwhelmed or stretched thin, don't hesitate to communicate your needs and seek support.

Practice Self-Care: Remember that taking care of yourself is essential for being present and available for your loved ones. Prioritize self-care activities that recharge you, whether it's exercise, meditation, hobbies, or simply taking time to relax. When you prioritize your well-being, you'll have more energy and enthusiasm to invest in your relationships.

By implementing these strategies, you can find a healthy balance between spending time with your family, friends, and colleagues. Remember that balance looks different for everyone, so be patient with yourself as you navigate your unique priorities and commitments. With intentionality and mindfulness, you can nurture meaningful connections in all areas of your life.

Strengthening Personal Relationships

Personal relationships form the foundation of our lives, providing us with love, support, and companionship through life's ups and downs. Whether it's our relationships with family members, friends, or romantic partners, nurturing these connections is essential for our overall well-being and happiness. In this section, we'll explore some simple yet powerful strategies for strengthening personal relationships and deepening the bonds we share with those we care about.

Communication is Key: Effective communication is the cornerstone of any healthy relationship. Take the time to listen actively to your loved ones, showing empathy and understanding. Express your thoughts and feelings openly and honestly, and encourage them to do the same. By communicating openly and authentically, you'll foster trust and intimacy in your relationships.

Quality Time Together: It is easy to get caught up in our own lives and neglect the people who matter most to us. Make a conscious effort to prioritize quality time with your loved ones, whether it's through shared activities, meaningful conversations, or simply enjoying each other's company. Carve out dedicated time in your schedule to connect with them regularly, and cherish these moments together.

Show Appreciation: Expressing gratitude and appreciation for the people in our lives can go a long way in strengthening our relationships. Take the time to acknowledge the efforts and contributions of your loved ones, and let them know how much they mean to you. Simple gestures like saying "thank you," writing a heartfelt note, or giving a thoughtful gift can make a world of difference and reinforce the bonds of love and affection.

Practice Empathy and Understanding: Empathy is the ability to understand and share the feelings of others, and it plays a crucial role in building strong relationships. Put yourself in the shoes of your loved ones and strive to see things from their perspective. Validate their emotions and experiences, even if you may not always agree with them. By practicing empathy and understanding, you'll foster deeper connections and mutual respect in your relationships.

Resolve Conflicts Constructively: Conflict is a natural part of any relationship, but it's how we handle it that determines the health and longevity of our connections. Instead of avoiding conflict or resorting to blame and criticism, approach disagreements with an open mind and a willingness to find common ground. Listen to each other's concerns, communicate calmly and respectfully, and work together to find mutually satisfactory solutions. By addressing conflicts constructively, you'll strengthen your relationship and build greater resilience together.

Cultivate Trust and Support: Trust forms the bedrock of any strong relationship, and it's essential to cultivate trust and support in your personal connections. Be reliable and dependable in your actions, and honor your commitments to your loved ones. Show them that they can count on you, both in good times and bad. Offer your unwavering support and encouragement, and be there for them when they need you most. By building trust and support, you'll create a solid foundation for a lasting and meaningful relationship.

Nurturing personal relationships is a lifelong journey that requires patience, effort, and commitment. By following all above, you can strengthen the bonds you share with your loved ones and create a foundation of love, happiness, and fulfillment in your life. Building strong relationships takes time and effort, but the rewards are immeasurable. So, invest in your relationships, cherish the moments you share, and watch as they blossom and thrive over time.

Networking and Social Support Systems

In our life, we encounter numerous people who play different roles, from colleagues and acquaintances to close friends and family members. These relationships form the fabric of our social support system, providing us with emotional, practical, and sometimes even professional support when we need it most.

Understanding Networking: Networking is more than just exchanging business cards or connecting with people on social media. It's about building genuine, meaningful relationships based on mutual respect, trust, and shared interests. Networking allows us to expand our social circle, meet new people, and tap into a wealth of resources and opportunities. Whether it's attending networking events, joining professional groups, or simply reaching out to old friends, networking opens doors and creates pathways for personal and professional growth.

Cultivating Social Support Systems: Our social support system consists of the people in our lives who offer us emotional support, encouragement, and practical assistance during challenging times. These may include family members, close friends, mentors, and colleagues who are there for us through thick and thin. Cultivating strong social support systems involves nurturing these relationships, being there for others when they need us, and building a network of trusted individuals we can rely on.

Benefits of Networking and Social Support Systems: Networking and social support systems offer a myriad of benefits that contribute to our overall well-being and happiness:

Emotional Support: During times of stress, uncertainty, or sadness, having a supportive network of friends and family members can provide comfort and reassurance.

Practical Assistance: From lending a listening ear to offering a helping hand, our social support system can help us navigate life's challenges more effectively.

Professional Opportunities: Networking opens doors to new job opportunities, collaborations, mentorships, and career advancements.

Increased Resilience: Knowing that we have a strong support system to fall back on can boost our resilience and ability to bounce back from setbacks.

Improved Health and Well-being: Studies have shown that individuals with strong social support systems tend to have better physical and mental health outcomes, lower levels of stress, and increased longevity.

Building and Maintaining Relationships: Building and maintaining relationships takes effort, time, and commitment. Here are some tips for nurturing relationships within your network:

Show genuine interest: Take the time to get to know the people in your network and show genuine interest in their lives, interests, and aspirations.

Be a good listener: Practice active listening and empathize with others' experiences and emotions.

Offer support: Be there for others when they need you, offering a listening ear, words of encouragement, or practical assistance whenever possible.

Stay connected: Regularly reach out to friends, family members, and colleagues to stay connected and maintain strong relationships.

Give back: Offer your support, knowledge, and expertise to others in your network, paying it forward and strengthening your bonds with them.

Leveraging Technology: Technology plays a significant role in how we connect and communicate with others. Social media platforms, messaging apps, and video conferencing tools make it easier than ever to stay in touch with friends, family, and colleagues, regardless of geographical distances. While technology can facilitate networking and social support, it's essential to strike a balance between online and offline interactions and prioritize meaningful, face-to-face connections whenever possible.

Maximizing Productivity

Maximizing productivity is essential for achieving success in both personal and professional endeavors. However, with so many demands on our time and attention, it can be challenging to know where to start. Fortunately, there are several effective strategies that can help us increase efficiency and productivity, allowing us to accomplish more in less time and with less stress.

Set Clear Goals: The first step in boosting productivity is to set clear and achievable goals. By clearly defining what you want to accomplish, you can create a roadmap for success and stay focused on your priorities. Whether it's completing a project at work, improving your health, or spending more time with loved ones, setting specific, measurable, and realistic goals is key to staying on track and making progress.

Prioritize Tasks: Not all tasks are created equal, and it's important to prioritize them based on their importance and urgency. Start by identifying the most critical tasks that require immediate attention and focus your energy on completing them first. Use tools like to-do lists or task management apps to organize your tasks and ensure that you're tackling the most important ones first.

Use Time Management Techniques: Effective time management is essential for maximizing productivity. Experiment with different techniques such as the Pomodoro Technique, time blocking, or the Eisenhower Matrix to find what works best for you. Set aside dedicated blocks of time for focused work, and be sure to schedule regular breaks to rest and recharge.

Minimize Distractions: Distractions can derail your productivity and make it difficult to stay focused on your tasks. Identify common distractions in your environment, such as social media, email, or noisy coworkers, and take steps to minimize them. Consider using productivity tools like website blockers or noise-canceling headphones to create a distraction-free work environment.

Delegate and Outsource: You don't have to do everything yourself. Learn to delegate tasks that can be done by others and focus your time and energy on activities that are most important and valuable to you. Whether it's assigning tasks to coworkers, hiring a virtual assistant, or outsourcing specific projects, delegating can help you free up time and resources for more meaningful work.

Streamline Processes: Look for ways to streamline your workflows and eliminate unnecessary steps or inefficiencies. Automate repetitive tasks using technology tools or create standardized processes to ensure consistency and efficiency. Continuously evaluate your workflows and identify areas for improvement to optimize your productivity over time.

Take Care of Yourself: Lastly, remember that productivity is not just about working harder—it's also about working smarter and taking care of yourself. Prioritize self-care activities such as exercise, adequate sleep, and healthy eating to maintain your physical and mental well-being. When you feel your best, you'll be better equipped to tackle challenges and stay productive throughout the day.

By implementing these strategies for increasing efficiency and productivity, you can take control of your time, accomplish more in less time, and ultimately, achieve greater success and fulfillment in all areas of your life. Experiment with different techniques, stay flexible, and don't be afraid to adjust your approach as needed. With dedication and perseverance, you can master productivity and unlock your full potential.

Avoiding Multitasking and Distractions

We often find ourselves trying to juggle multiple tasks at once, believing that it will help us get more done in less time. However, the reality is that multitasking can actually decrease our productivity and make it harder for us to focus on the task at hand. In addition, constant distractions, such as phone notifications, emails, and social media, can further hinder our ability to concentrate and complete tasks efficiently.

To maximize productivity, it's essential to avoid multitasking and minimize distractions as much as possible. Here are some simple strategies to help you stay focused and on track:

Prioritize Your Tasks: Start by identifying the most important tasks that need to be completed each day. Prioritize these tasks based on their urgency and importance, and focus on completing one task at a time before moving on to the next.

Create a Dedicated Workspace: Designate a specific area in your home or office where you can work without distractions. Make sure this space is free from clutter and noise, and set up your workstation in a way that allows you to focus fully on your work.

Set Clear Boundaries: Establish boundaries with yourself and others to minimize distractions during work hours. Turn off unnecessary notifications on your phone and computer, and let friends and family know that you are not available for non-urgent matters during certain times of the day.

Use Time Blocking: Allocate specific blocks of time for different tasks throughout your day. Schedule time for focused work, as well as breaks for rest and relaxation. Stick to your schedule as much as possible to maintain a sense of structure and routine.

Practice Mindfulness: Stay present and focused on the task at hand by practicing mindfulness techniques, such as deep breathing or meditation. Whenever you notice your mind wandering or getting distracted, gently bring your attention back to the present moment.

Limit Multitasking: Resist the temptation to multitask, as it can actually decrease your efficiency and lead to more errors. Instead, focus on completing one task at a time with full attention and dedication.

Take Regular Breaks: Give yourself permission to take short breaks throughout the day to rest and recharge. Use this time to stretch, go for a walk, or engage in activities that help you relax and clear your mind.

Use Tools and Apps: Leverage technology to help you stay focused and organized. Use productivity apps to create to-do lists, set reminders, and track your progress on tasks. Consider using website blockers or apps that limit your access to distracting websites and social media platforms during work hours.

By implementing these strategies and making a conscious effort to avoid multitasking and minimize distractions, you can enhance your productivity, improve your focus, and achieve greater success in both your personal and professional life. Productivity is not about doing more tasks at once, but rather about doing fewer tasks with greater efficiency and effectiveness.

Creating a Conducive Work Environment for Maximizing Productivity

In the quest to maximize productivity, creating a conducive work environment plays a crucial role. A conducive work environment refers to the physical, social, and cultural conditions within a workplace that support employee well-being, engagement, and effectiveness. When employees feel comfortable, motivated, and valued in their work environment, they are more likely to perform at their best and contribute positively to the organization's success.

Here are some key elements to consider when creating a conducive work environment:

Physical Comfort: Providing comfortable and ergonomic workstations can significantly impact employee productivity and well-being. This includes ergonomic chairs, adjustable desks, proper lighting, and adequate ventilation. Ensuring a clean and clutter-free workspace can also help reduce distractions and promote focus.

Open Communication: Fostering open communication channels between management and employees is essential for creating a positive work environment. Employees should feel comfortable expressing their ideas, concerns, and feedback without fear of reprisal. Regular team meetings, one-on-one sessions with managers, and anonymous suggestion boxes can facilitate open communication and collaboration.

Work-Life Balance: Encouraging work-life balance is vital for employee satisfaction and retention. Providing flexible work arrangements, such as telecommuting options or flexible hours, allows employees to better manage their personal and professional responsibilities. Additionally, offering wellness programs, onsite childcare, or employee assistance programs can support employees in achieving a healthy work-life balance.

Recognition and Rewards: Recognizing and rewarding employee contributions can boost morale and motivation in the workplace. Implementing a formal recognition program to acknowledge employee achievements, milestones, and exceptional performance can foster a culture of appreciation and recognition. This can include awards, bonuses, public acknowledgment, or opportunities for career advancement.

Clear Expectations: Setting clear expectations and goals for employees helps create a sense of purpose and direction. Employees should understand their roles, responsibilities, and performance expectations. Providing regular feedback and performance evaluations can help employees track their progress and make necessary adjustments to meet organizational goals.

Training and Development: Investing in employee training and development programs demonstrates a commitment to employee growth and professional advancement. Offering opportunities for skill development, continuing education, and career advancement can enhance employee engagement and job satisfaction. This can include workshops, seminars, online courses, mentorship programs, or tuition reimbursement.

Team Collaboration: Encouraging collaboration and teamwork among employees promotes creativity, innovation, and problem-solving. Creating collaborative workspaces, organizing team-building activities, and fostering a culture of cooperation can strengthen relationships and enhance productivity. Emphasizing the value of diversity and inclusion can also enrich team dynamics and foster a supportive work environment.

Wellness Initiatives: Prioritizing employee health and well-being is essential for maintaining a productive workforce. Implementing wellness initiatives, such as health screenings, fitness challenges, mental health resources, and stress management programs, can support employee wellness and reduce absenteeism. Providing access to healthy snacks, hydration stations, and designated break areas can also promote physical and mental well-being.

Empowerment and Autonomy: Empowering employees with autonomy and decision-making authority can increase job satisfaction and engagement. Allowing employees to take ownership of their work, make decisions, and contribute ideas fosters a sense of ownership and accountability. Providing opportunities for autonomy encourages creativity, innovation, and problem-solving.

Continuous Improvement: Cultivating a culture of continuous improvement encourages employees to seek opportunities for growth, learning, and innovation. Encouraging experimentation, risk-taking, and learning from failures promotes adaptability and resilience. Implementing processes for gathering feedback, conducting regular performance evaluations, and identifying areas for improvement ensures ongoing growth and development.

Creating a conducive work environment is essential for maximizing productivity, fostering employee engagement, and driving organizational success. By prioritizing physical comfort, open communication, work-life balance, recognition and rewards, clear expectations, training and development, team collaboration, wellness initiatives, empowerment, and continuous improvement, organizations can create a positive and supportive workplace culture where employees thrive and excel.

Flexibility and Adaptability

One of the most valuable skills we can cultivate is the ability to embrace change and unpredictability. Rather than resisting or fearing the unknown, adopting a mindset of flexibility and adaptability allows us to navigate life's twists and turns with grace and resilience.

Change is an inevitable part of life, and it comes in many forms – from changes in our personal circumstances to shifts in our professional environments. While change can be daunting, it also presents us with opportunities for growth, learning, and new experiences. By embracing change rather than resisting it, we open ourselves up to the possibility of positive transformation and personal development.

Similarly, unpredictability is a fact of life that we must learn to accept and adapt to. The future is inherently uncertain, and we cannot control every outcome or circumstance. Instead of trying to predict or control the future, we can cultivate a mindset of openness and flexibility, allowing us to respond effectively to whatever life throws our way.

Flexibility and adaptability enable us to thrive in the face of uncertainty and change. Rather than clinging to rigid plans or expectations, we learn to go with the flow, adjusting our approach as needed to meet the demands of the present moment. This mindset allows us to remain resilient in the face of challenges, setbacks, and unexpected events.

So, how can we cultivate greater flexibility and adaptability in our lives? It starts with shifting our mindset and embracing a willingness to embrace change and uncertainty. Instead of viewing change as a threat, we can see it as an opportunity for growth and evolution. By staying open-minded, curious, and adaptable, we can navigate life's twists and turns with greater ease and confidence.

Practical strategies for cultivating flexibility and adaptability include:

Cultivating a Growth Mindset: Embrace challenges as opportunities for growth and learning. Adopt a positive attitude towards change and view setbacks as valuable learning experiences.

Practicing Mindfulness: Stay present in the moment and cultivate awareness of your thoughts, feelings, and reactions. Mindfulness allows you to respond to situations with greater clarity and intention.

Remaining Open-Minded: Be willing to consider alternative perspectives and approaches. Avoid rigid thinking and be open to new ideas, feedback, and possibilities.

Building Resilience: Develop resilience by building strong social connections, practicing self-care, and developing coping skills to manage stress and adversity.

Embracing Uncertainty: Accept that uncertainty is a natural part of life and practice letting go of the need for control. Trust in your ability to adapt and thrive in the face of the unknown.

By embracing change and unpredictability with an open heart and mind, we can cultivate greater resilience, flexibility, and adaptability in our lives.

Rather than fearing the unknown, we can embrace it as an opportunity for growth, learning, and personal transformation.

Developing Resilience in the Face of Challenges

In life, we often encounter unexpected challenges and obstacles that can shake us to our core. Whether it's a sudden setback at work, a personal loss, or a global crisis, our ability to adapt and bounce back in the face of adversity is crucial for maintaining our well-being and moving forward with strength and resilience.

Understanding Resilience:

Resilience is the ability to withstand and bounce back from adversity, challenges, and setbacks. It's not about avoiding difficult situations altogether, but rather about facing them head-on and emerging stronger and more capable as a result. Resilience is like a muscle that can be strengthened through practice and perseverance.

Factors Contributing to Resilience:

Positive Mindset: Cultivating a positive outlook on life can help us see challenges as opportunities for growth and learning. Instead of dwelling on the negatives, we can focus on finding solutions and maintaining hope for the future.

Social Support: Building strong connections with friends, family, and community can provide a valuable source of emotional support during tough times. Having a network of people who care about us and are willing to lend a listening ear can make all the difference in our ability to cope with challenges.

Problem-Solving Skills: Developing effective problem-solving skills allows us to approach challenges in a systematic and strategic manner. By breaking down complex problems into smaller, more manageable tasks, we can find practical solutions and take proactive steps toward overcoming adversity.

Adaptability: Flexibility and adaptability are essential qualities for resilience. Being able to adjust our plans and expectations in response to changing circumstances allows us to navigate challenges more effectively and find creative solutions to unexpected problems.

Self-Compassion: Practicing self-compassion involves treating ourselves with kindness and understanding, especially during difficult times. By acknowledging our own humanity and accepting our imperfections, we can cultivate greater resilience and bounce back from setbacks with greater ease.

Developing Resilience:

Cultivate Optimism: Practice gratitude, focus on the positive aspects of life, and maintain hope for the future, even in the face of challenges.

Build Strong Relationships: Invest time and effort in nurturing supportive relationships with friends, family, and colleagues who uplift and encourage you.

Enhance Problem-Solving Skills: Seek out opportunities to develop your problem-solving abilities through practice, learning from past experiences, and seeking feedback from others.

Embrace Change: Instead of resisting change, learn to embrace it as an opportunity for growth and transformation. Stay flexible and open-minded in your approach to life.

Practice Self-Care: Prioritize your physical, emotional, and mental well-being by engaging in activities that nourish and rejuvenate you, such as exercise, meditation, and hobbies.

Seek Support: Don't be afraid to reach out for help when you need it. Whether it's talking to a trusted friend, seeking guidance from a mentor, or seeking professional support, there are resources available to support you through difficult times.

By cultivating resilience in the face of challenges, we can build the inner strength and fortitude needed to navigate life's ups and downs with grace and courage. Remember that resilience is not about avoiding adversity, but about facing it with courage, perseverance, and a belief in our own ability to overcome.

Learning to adapt and adjust priorities as needed:

One of the essential skills to cultivate is flexibility and adaptability. Life is unpredictable, and circumstances often change without warning. Therefore, it's crucial to be able to adapt and adjust our priorities accordingly to navigate through the ups and downs of daily life.

Flexibility means being open to change and willing to embrace new ways of doing things. It's about having a mindset that is agile and resilient, capable of bending without breaking when faced with unexpected challenges or opportunities. In the context of work-life balance, flexibility allows us to respond effectively to shifting demands and responsibilities, ensuring that we can meet our obligations without sacrificing our well-being or personal happiness.

Adaptability goes hand in hand with flexibility, as it involves not only being open to change but also actively responding to it in a constructive manner. This means being able to assess situations quickly, identify the necessary adjustments, and take proactive steps to implement them. Whether it's reorganizing our schedules, reallocating resources, or renegotiating priorities, adaptability enables us to find creative solutions to overcome obstacles and achieve our goals.

So, how can we cultivate flexibility and adaptability in our lives? Here are some practical tips to consider:

Embrace the mindset of "go with the flow": Instead of rigidly clinging to specific plans or expectations, adopt a more fluid approach to life. Recognize that things may not always go according to plan, and that's okay. By letting go of the need for control and learning to embrace uncertainty, you can navigate through life's twists and turns with greater ease.

Practice mindfulness: Mindfulness involves being fully present in the moment and non-judgmentally aware of your thoughts, feelings, and surroundings. By cultivating mindfulness, you can develop greater self-awareness and emotional resilience, enabling you to respond to situations with calmness and clarity rather than reactively.

Stay adaptable in your routines: While routines can provide structure and stability, it's essential to remain flexible and open to adjusting them as needed. Be willing to experiment with different approaches to managing your time and tasks, and don't be afraid to deviate from your usual routines if they no longer serve you.

Prioritize self-care: Taking care of yourself is essential for maintaining the resilience and energy needed to adapt to life's challenges. Make self-care a non-negotiable part of your routine, whether it's through exercise, meditation, spending time with loved ones, or engaging in activities that bring you joy.

Build a support network: Surround yourself with people who uplift and support you, both personally and professionally. A strong support network can provide invaluable encouragement, guidance, and perspective during times of change or uncertainty.

By cultivating flexibility and adaptability in our lives, we can navigate through the complexities of work-life balance with greater ease and resilience. Instead of being overwhelmed by change, we can embrace it as an opportunity for growth and transformation. So, let's commit to embracing flexibility and adaptability in our lives and mastering the art of work-life balance.

Self-Reflection and Growth

It is easy to get caught up in the whirlwind of tasks, responsibilities, and distractions. The path to self-reflection and growth begins with a commitment to continuous learning and application of learning throughout our life.

Practicing mindfulness and self-awareness

Taking the time to cultivate mindfulness and self-awareness can be incredibly beneficial for our overall well being and personal growth. Let's explore how practicing mindfulness and self-awareness can help us navigate life with greater clarity, peace, and purpose.

Mindfulness is the practice of being fully present in the moment, without judgment or attachment to thoughts, emotions, or sensations. It involves paying attention to our thoughts, feelings, and surroundings with curiosity and openness. By bringing our awareness to the present moment, we can cultivate a sense of calm, clarity, and inner peace.

One way to cultivate mindfulness is through the practice of meditation. Meditation involves sitting quietly and focusing on the breath, sensations in the body, or a specific object of attention. Through regular meditation practice, we can train our minds to become more focused, resilient, and present in our daily lives.

Another way to cultivate mindfulness is by bringing awareness to our daily activities and routines. Whether it's eating a meal, taking a walk, or washing the dishes, we can practice mindfulness by fully engaging in the present moment and savoring the experience. By bringing mindfulness to our daily activities, we can enhance our appreciation for the simple joys of life and reduce stress and anxiety.

Self-awareness, on the other hand, involves recognizing and understanding our thoughts, emotions, and behaviors. It's about being honest with ourselves and acknowledging our strengths, weaknesses, and areas for growth. Cultivating self-awareness allows us to make more informed choices, develop healthier habits, and cultivate deeper connections with ourselves and others.

One way to cultivate self-awareness is through self-reflection. Taking time to journal, meditate, or simply sit quietly and reflect on our thoughts and experiences can help us gain insight into our inner world. By examining our thoughts, emotions, and patterns of behavior, we can uncover underlying beliefs and motivations and make positive changes in our lives.Another way to cultivate self-awareness is by seeking feedback from others. Asking for honest feedback from friends, family members, or colleagues can provide valuable insights into our strengths and areas for improvement By remaining open to feedback and willing to learn and grow, we can become more self-aware and better equipped to navigate life's challenges.

Practicing mindfulness and self-awareness can have profound benefits for our overall well-being and personal growth. By cultivating mindfulness, we can learn to live more fully in the present moment and experience greater peace and happiness. By cultivating self-awareness, we can gain insight into ourselves and make positive changes that lead to greater fulfillment and success in life. So let's commit to practicing mindfulness and self-awareness each day, and watch as our lives unfold with greater clarity, purpose, and joy.

Reflecting on Values and Goals Regularly

Self-reflection is a powerful tool for personal growth and development. By taking the time to pause and examine our values and goals regularly, we can gain valuable insights into our priorities, aspirations, and the direction we want our lives to take.

Understanding Values: Values are the guiding principles that shape our beliefs, attitudes, and behaviors. They represent what is most important to us and serve as a compass for decision-making. Reflecting on our values allows us to ensure that our actions align with what truly matters to us. It's essential to take the time to identify our core values and reflect on whether our current lifestyle and choices are in harmony with them.

Examining Goals: Goals are the milestones we set for ourselves to achieve our desired outcomes. They provide direction and motivation, helping us to progress and grow. Regularly reflecting on our goals allows us to assess our progress, celebrate our achievements, and adjust our course if necessary. It's important to ask ourselves whether our goals are still relevant, realistic, and aligned with our values and priorities.

Benefits of Regular Reflection:

Clarity: Regular reflection helps clarify our values and goals, allowing us to gain a deeper understanding of ourselves and what we want to achieve.

Alignment: By aligning our actions with our values and goals, we can lead more authentic and purposeful lives.

Growth: Reflection fosters personal growth and development by encouraging us to learn from our experiences, both successes, and failures.

Adaptability: Regularly reflecting on our values and goals enables us to adapt to changing circumstances and adjust our plans accordingly.

Well-being: Reflecting on our values and goals can enhance our overall well-being by promoting self-awareness, resilience, and satisfaction with life.

Practical Tips for Reflection:

Schedule regular reflection sessions: Set aside dedicated time each week or month to reflect on your values and goals.

Journaling: Keep a journal to record your thoughts, insights, and reflections. Writing can help clarify your thoughts and feelings.

Meditation and mindfulness: Practice mindfulness techniques to quiet the mind and cultivate self-awareness. Meditation can help you connect with your values and goals on a deeper level.

Seek feedback: Ask trusted friends, family members, or mentors for feedback on your progress and areas for improvement.

Celebrate progress: Take time to celebrate your achievements and milestones along the way. Celebrating progress can boost motivation and reinforce positive behaviors.

Regularly reflecting on our values and goals is a powerful practice that can lead to greater clarity, alignment, and personal growth. By taking the time to pause and examine what truly matters to us, we can live more meaningful and fulfilling lives. Incorporate these practical tips into your routine and make reflection a regular habit. Remember, the journey of self-discovery and growth begins with a moment of reflection.

Continuous Learning and Personal Development

Self-reflection and growth are like the wind beneath our wings, propelling us forward toward our fullest potential. At the heart of this journey lies the concept of continuous learning and personal development, a process that empowers us to evolve, adapt, and thrive in an ever-changing world.

Continuous learning is more than just acquiring new skills or knowledge; it's a mindset—an insatiable curiosity that drives us to seek out new experiences, ideas, and perspectives. It's about embracing every opportunity as a chance to grow, to expand our horizons, and to challenge ourselves to become better versions of who we are.

But what does continuous learning look like in practice? It's about setting aside time each day to read a book, listen to a podcast, or take an online course. It's about seeking out mentors and experts who can share their wisdom and guidance with us. It's about staying open-minded and humble, recognizing that there is always something new to learn and someone new to learn from.

Personal development, on the other hand, is about taking intentional steps to improve ourselves—physically, mentally, emotionally, and spiritually. It's about setting goals, developing healthy habits, and cultivating a growth mindset that sees challenges as opportunities for growth rather than obstacles to overcome.

One of the keys to personal development is self-awareness—knowing ourselves deeply, understanding our strengths and weaknesses, and recognizing our patterns of behavior. Through self-reflection, we can gain insight into our thoughts, feelings, and actions, allowing us to make more conscious choices and take more intentional steps toward our goals.

But personal development is not just about self-improvement; it's also about self-acceptance and self-compassion. It's about embracing our flaws and imperfections, recognizing that they are an integral part of what makes us human. It's about treating ourselves with kindness and compassion, even when we fall short of our own expectations.

Incorporating continuous learning and personal development into our lives requires commitment and consistency. It's not always easy, and there will inevitably be obstacles along the way. But by staying focused on our goals, staying true to ourselves, and staying open to new possibilities, we can continue to grow and evolve, becoming the best versions of ourselves in the process.

On your own journey of self-reflection and growth, always follow the process, celebrate your progress, and keep moving forward, one step at a time. The path to personal fulfillment and self-actualization begins with a commitment to continuous learning and personal development, and the possibilities are endless.

Implementing Work-Life Balance

Balancing work and life proves challenging across various life stages due to the unpredictable nature of challenges that life presents.

Balancing Work and Personal Life During Different Life Stages

Navigating the delicate balance between work and personal life is a journey that evolves as we progress through different stages of life. Each stage presents its own unique challenges and opportunities, requiring us to adapt and find new ways to maintain harmony and fulfillment in both spheres. Let's explore how to balance work and personal life during three key life stages: early career, parenthood, and retirement.

Early Career:

In the early stages of our career, the focus is often on establishing ourselves professionally and building a strong foundation for the future. This may involve long hours, intense workloads, and a relentless pursuit of career advancement.

While dedication to our careers is important, it's equally crucial to prioritize self-care and personal development. Setting boundaries around work hours, taking regular breaks, and pursuing hobbies and interests outside of work can help maintain a healthy work-life balance.

Investing in professional growth through continued education, networking, and skill development can open up new opportunities for career advancement while also enriching our personal lives.

Parenthood:

Parenthood brings a whole new set of responsibilities and challenges, as we strive to balance the demands of work with the needs of our family. Juggling childcare, school activities, and household chores alongside work commitments can feel overwhelming at times.

Communication and collaboration with our employers and colleagues are key during this stage.

Negotiating flexible work arrangements, such as remote work options or adjusted schedules, can provide greater flexibility to meet both work and family obligations.

Prioritizing quality time with family, establishing routines, and seeking support from partners, family members, and childcare providers can help alleviate stress and create a more balanced and harmonious family life.

Retirement:

Retirement marks a significant transition from the structured routines of work to a newfound freedom and leisure. While retirement offers the opportunity to pursue personal interests and hobbies, it also requires careful planning and adjustment.

Finding purpose and meaning in retirement can be achieved through volunteer work, pursuing lifelong passions, or embarking on new adventures. Maintaining social connections and staying active physically and mentally are essential for overall well-being.

Embracing retirement as a time for self-discovery, personal growth, and fulfillment allows us to create a balanced and fulfilling life that is rich in experiences and meaningful connections.

In short, balancing work and personal life is a dynamic process that evolves over time. By recognizing the unique challenges and opportunities presented by different life stages and adopting strategies for self-reflection and growth, we can navigate these transitions with grace and resilience, leading to a more fulfilling and balanced life overall.

Adjusting Strategies Based on Changing Circumstances

One of the most valuable skills we can develop is the ability to adjust our strategies based on changing circumstances. Life is full of twists and turns, and what worked for us yesterday may not necessarily work for us tomorrow. Therefore, it's essential to remain flexible and adaptable in our approach to achieving our goals and aspirations.

Here are some key insights and practical tips:

Embrace Change: Change is inevitable, and resisting it only leads to frustration and stagnation. Instead of fearing change, embrace it as an opportunity for growth and transformation. By adopting a mindset of flexibility and openness, you can more effectively navigate the ever-changing landscape of life.

Stay Agile: Just as a ship adjusts its course in response to changing winds, we must learn to stay agile and responsive to the shifting tides of life. This means being willing to let go of rigid plans and expectations and instead, remain open to new possibilities and opportunities that may arise unexpectedly.

Assess Your Situation: Regularly take stock of your current circumstances and assess whether your current strategies are still serving you effectively. Are there any new challenges or obstacles that have emerged? Are there any opportunities that you may have overlooked? By regularly evaluating your situation, you can identify areas where adjustments may be necessary.

Be Willing to Pivot: Sometimes, despite our best efforts, things don't go as planned. In such instances, it's important to be willing to pivot and change course if necessary. This may involve shifting your priorities, revising your goals, or exploring new approaches to achieving them. Remember, flexibility is the key to resilience.

Learn from Setbacks: Setbacks and failures are inevitable parts of life, but they also present valuable learning opportunities. Instead of viewing setbacks as roadblocks, see them as stepping stones on the path to success. Take the time to reflect on what went wrong, what lessons you can learn from the experience, and how you can adjust your strategies moving forward.

Seek Feedback: Don't hesitate to seek feedback from others, whether it's from mentors, peers, or trusted advisors. External perspectives can offer valuable insights and help you identify blind spots that you may not have been aware of. Be open to constructive criticism and use it as fuel for growth and improvement.

Practice Adaptability: Adaptability is a skill that can be cultivated through practice. Challenge yourself to step outside of your comfort zone, try new things, and embrace unfamiliar situations. The more you expose yourself to change, the more comfortable you will become with adapting to it.

Stay Committed to Your Values: While it's important to be flexible in your approach, it's equally important to stay true to your core values and principles. Your values serve as your guiding light, helping you navigate through life's ups and downs with integrity and authenticity. No matter how much your circumstances may change, let your values be your anchor.

Adjusting strategies based on changing circumstances is an essential aspect of self-reflection and growth. By remaining flexible, agile, and adaptable, you can navigate life's twists and turns with grace and resilience. Embrace change as an opportunity for growth, assess your situation regularly, be willing to pivot when necessary, and stay committed to your values. Life is a journey, and learning to adjust your course along the way is all part of the adventure.

Final Thoughts

As we come to the end of this journey towards mastering work-life balance, it's essential to reflect on the insights gained and the transformation experienced along the way. Achieving harmony between our professional and personal lives is not just about managing our time more effectively or setting boundaries; it's about fostering a mindset of holistic well-being and aligning our actions with our values and priorities.

Throughout this book, we have explored various strategies and techniques for navigating the complexities of modern life while maintaining a sense of balance and fulfillment. From setting clear boundaries and priorities to practicing self-care and mindfulness, each lesson has been a stepping stone towards creating a life that feels meaningful and purposeful.

But perhaps the most important lesson of all is the realization that true fulfillment doesn't come from external achievements or accolades but from within.

It's about cultivating a deep sense of self-awareness and authenticity, honoring our unique strengths and passions, and living in alignment with our core values.

As we strive to integrate our professional aspirations with our personal goals and relationships, it's crucial to remember that balance is not a destination but a continuous journey. It requires constant adjustment and recalibration as our circumstances and priorities evolve over time.

Along the way, it's essential to seek support and guidance from mentors, colleagues, friends, and family members who can offer perspective, encouragement, and accountability. Building a strong support network and surrounding ourselves with positive influences can make all the difference in our ability to navigate life's challenges and stay true to our vision of balance and fulfillment.

In the pursuit of work-life balance, it's also important to embrace the concept of imperfection and self-compassion. We will inevitably encounter setbacks, obstacles, and moments of overwhelm along the way, and that's okay. What matters most is our ability to bounce back, learn from our experiences, and continue moving forward with resilience and determination.

Ultimately, achieving work-life balance is not about striving for perfection or achieving some arbitrary standard of success; it's about living authentically and intentionally, embracing the full spectrum of our human experience, and finding joy and fulfillment in the everyday moments that matter most.

So, as you travel on your journey towards mastering work-life balance, I encourage you to approach it with curiosity, openness, and a spirit of adventure. Remember that you have the power to create a life that reflects your deepest desires and aspirations, and that true fulfillment lies not in the destination but in the journey itself.

With dedication, self-awareness, and a commitment to living in alignment with your values and priorities, you have the potential to create a life of meaning, purpose, and profound fulfillment in both your work and personal life. The possibilities are endless, and the journey is yours to embrace.

*Please scan for the other books of the **"Life Mastery"** Series.*

Other References

1) Free Courses
2) Join my Community
3) Want to be the Online Coach?

www.ingramcontent.com/pod-product-compliance
Lightning Source LLC
Chambersburg PA
CBHW050118230526
45470CB00004B/1893

Investeren in Vastgoed in Spanje: Een Complete Gids

Wil je investeren in vastgoed in Spanje? Deze gids biedt je alle informatie die je nodig hebt, van de beste locaties en strategieën tot belastingen en regelgeving. Perfect voor zowel beginnende als ervaren investeerders.
